In the Service of Time

In the Service of Time

Roselle M. Lewis

To order additional copies of this book, contact:
Xlibris Corporation
1-888-795-4274
www.Xlibris.com
Orders@Xlibris.com
26275

CONTENTS

In The Service Of Time 7

The Unsolid Flesh 9

Winter Dream 11

Long Distance..12

In The Ante Room Of Decision 13

Night Ward 15

Menses 16

In Flight...17

Of Generation 18

At Seventy 19

Miracle Man 20

Birthday Letter "Il faut d'abord durer." 21

At A Neighbor's Funeral...22

Apollo 24

At The Exhibit 25

Into Morning...26

Horses Of The Night 27

A Question...28

Gettysburg...29

Die Zeitung 30

Off The Miramar 31

January First..32

Self Portrait: The basement ladies room, Royce Hall, UCLA 33

Three Farewells 35

Possessor Of The House 39

Memoriam: May, 1975 40

Odd Tributaries 41

    The Turtle Song 42

    Mother's Credo 43

The Gift 44

I Lost It At The Movies 45

Let The Night Creep In 46

A Just Reward 47

After Her Funeral 48

In The Service Of Time

Winter claims New Haven's cemetery
Public to the private few straying
Its ice-iron paths, white leafless ways
In cold and curious memory
Of their strict sere lives that do lie
Down beneath our treading feet.
Oh, hugger-mugger winds of time
Have laid their darling bones in place,
And pagan souls are fired to know
That hell-mad Preacher Edwards
Once mused his widowed student way
Down this self-same lane, a cinder
Of spiders leaping into flame.

In Gothic towers across the way,
The young, enchanted by anatomy,
Play the cats cradle of disbelief,
Scorn this chock-a-block of names.
But stones are monuments to memory.
They speak of Allerton, first Mayflower man
Pilgrimed in his once-new earth who sleeps
Close by to Atwater and Phipps, Allen and Gibbs
In company with Anne, Susan and Jane,
Mehitabel, too, spoused in long testimony.

Know that Elihu Sanford found furious glory
With Mistress Howell, both dwelling now
With two lost babes in quietest ways,
While naked angels eye eternity
And sing them songs of faithful bliss.

Their spent passion, their vacant flesh speak"
   "For to me to live is Christ
   And to die is gain."
Here is rest and peace and vast belief
Dark years turning on darkening snow,
The light fails among incised grief.
They believed, they know with certainty
What we in formless freedom will never know.
Here at the edge of time, I bend closer to see.
Though marble wears better, they've used mere stone,
Wearing those grave names down to the bone.

¶

The Unsolid Flesh

Nightgowned in Macbethian scheme
You rubbed white palms into red,
Played it out incarnadined
Before leaping into that well-made bed.
Life, that huge thing, overlooks the fears
And simple vices of all our every days.
Isn't that what Emilia whispers
To willow singing Desdemon as she prays?
Yet, you three with Atropean shears
Went snip, snap, snout—quick rout!

Sylvia, in your bee-hived distress
Brewed up a vulgar poisonous mess,
Leaving your ill-mapped maze
To buzz over fecund sunless days.
Then pop, flower head into waiting oven,
A captured Hansel, but still a dozen
Witches thrive from this tale quite heedless.

Anne, you also tracked the bees
In dark rumination, honeyed unhealth,
Breathed the hose end of perfumed stealth
Brought untold ecstasies.

You, Virginia, with much-touted vision
Weighted your skirts at the river's flow,
Lying to Leonard—"The rhododendron"
In comical reversal of high-windowed reason,
No "mens sana en corpore sano."

Poets, you hurled away the gods' brave gift,
A frivolous toy tossed into the trash.
Once may prove time enough to sift
Brightness and beauty from the ash:
Still, once is all we can demand
From running waters and shifting sand.

Now solemn alienists, what do you say
To these cases of goodbye and grave turn away?

¶

Winter Dream

In Tolstoy's Anna, the skating rink
Mirrors fiction's dream, the coldest truth.
There dwells Levin, his dark Russian hope
Bearded with superstition; he prays
To the skater's music that Kitty
Will put on his passion, sinewy love.
She will entangle his man's thing
With petticoats and lace, knit his dream
Into skeins of children and leapfrog
With fruitful flowers into seduced seasons.
His hope of perfection is drowned
In the white coming night and
In full flood that his will be done.

¶

Long Distance

He calls, a shade under twenty
   across the continent east to west.
I've memorized his animal-length hair,
   scent for sure, gamey body meant
   for some strange woman's future love.
His voice surprises in its upward slopes;
   his fingers molded from my clay
   strum the window still impatiently,   -
   blind to his world of wintered snow,
   the storms and drifts over empty miles.
My words, laughable antique fables,
   injunctions on coats and time tables
   fall into chasms of disbelief.
Wrung once from my loins in loud distress,
   pain tamed into part forgetfulness,
   today he masters my servant title,
   mistress of packages and clean clothes,
   my role cloddishly maternal.
While other men find me toothsome still
   "une femme d'une certain age,"
   he takes note in the modern way,
   a bird's eye love, safe and sanitary.
As I shudder over the mess at Thebes,
And like that dark queen aim to please.

§

In The Ante Room Of Decision

T hey hiss like pious geese
 Deliver yourself brown and whole,
Intact package to the magician's door.

Ho, surgeon, you of blue cross
Honors, your waxed smile predicts
Strange uncertain growths
Thriving in mushroom darkness.
It is like the moon's unseen side.
It does not wax, it does not wane.

I nod cool, heroine brave
To authority set in golden seals
That mocks old Greek's translated oath.
In your statistical eyes dollars
Balloon like a cartoon message:
"Excise, excise, it is wise."

Body and blood brew a case from
Your just-memorized journal.
The prognosis of my blue whirl of time,
Ah, grains of months, seeds of years.

I nod cool, soldier brave.
When I present myself to lie down
Cautious volunteer to darkness,
The clouds of memory will ooze,
Water drawn to the lips of sky
On a summer's day of fervid heat.
I will be rowed by strangers to a far shore,
Land of alien hues and cries.

Now tan from your Mexican vacation,
Bastard son of Asculapius,
Having brought all you know from
The false bottom of your black art,
Inflict a legal rape,
Leave your proud scar like the line,
Of the horizon where sea and sky
Are severed and mend.

Must I agree and sign
A lifetime contract to awake
In a pre-paid, flower-cloyed room,
To share the cozy camaraderie of pain
With some deformed white-bedded stranger?

Together we will litanize our invalid griefs,
Nod cool and brave,
Scarred specimens of our kind
Sacrificed to the snake's art.

¶

Night Ward

On the frontier to this unsurveyed city,
A previous tourist, inevitable fat lady
Halted by underpaid, indifferent guards
Reveals her baggage: stomach gurglings
Unmundified bedpan banter.
She empties the portmanteau
Of belch and burp.

Pain that in some can be useful
In her grows to cabbage leaf complaint.
Her Bow Bells vowels peal like
Dawn's sick weathercock,
Doodles of rot, her so-ho gaseous
Balloons crisscross my surgical sky.

And having loved all music of speech,
I worry to wake again and hear
The purity of word, the forgiveness
That language alone can lend.

¶

Menses

The gourd of days is filled with watery grief,
     Knotted plaints, rusted disorders
Leap into the tidal bay of her mouth.
The gods are shriven and turn to stone.
She speaks of his Shiva-eyed mother,
Hers by law, some friend's lip-lash slight,
Another's success in the marketplace,
The dollar that dwindles, the song that slumps.

The land is lunar burned by
Infertile sun to cold craters where
Grasses cringe, flowers lose fury
And small morning birds are silent.

At last the rains of terror run dry.
In the bruised, battered silence
Against the dependable western sky
Mounts the thin sickle of moon.

¶

In Flight

L and grant America unfurls its geography
  That reads simple as a primer
Or puzzle for slow children. Find Kansas,
That flat pancake right in the middle
Of this fake put-together continent.
Pilot Jones, in rehearsed statistics,
Talks about highs and lows, flight info.
But we are too far above rocks and rills
For viewing earthly delights.
Next to me, a strapped experimented upon monkey,
My fellow citizen takes his food and drink
From plastic tubes and reads Americanese.
He sells something real—plastics or furs;
Dark, depressed, blowing old faithful cigar smoke
He is orthodox in his traditional vices.
I regret not smuggling a gun aboard
For the hell of scrambling security.
But how?
In the lavy I could carve a .45 from soap
Stain it Dick Tracy black,
Skyjack us all the way to heaven.

¶

Of Generation

My mother's mother stole last night,
absconding with clear day-filled dreams,
uncurled her ladder of brown hair,
descended to my tale of generation.
Once, from my mother's bewildered bureau drawer,
I found her photoed flower face,
eyes of captured deer, lips in dim distaste:
same soul, same prayer, same race.
In her new land of promised milk and honey,
she sold shoelaces in the snow;
school children sneered at her speech,
altered to moneyed syllables,
patois of broken dishes, bed, chairs.
In dreamland second hand America,
she moved with recalled shtetl truths:
skirts hemmed with pogrom mud,
hands chicken red, blood and feather white;
stripped on occasions of the moon
to be purged by mikvah water rites,
made fit for her master's strong delights.
From his tyrant's seed seven daughters of
of biblical despair, the act of sacrifice:
To be a woman is a vice.
Last night in the raw light of my new west,
I, grandmother's brown-haired issue,
raved on the narrow stage of dawn,
dressed in the cerements of rage.
I know a decayed old world soul,
know we are the same woman of the dream.

¶

At Seventy

Today she is old, old at last,
Old blood pulsing to false applied cheeks
Piqued by shots of vitamin B,
Eyes outlined for her heavy day.

Remembering when I was a girl galaxies ago,
How she set out pots to catch winter leaks,
Waxed "her" wooden floors on bended knees
At the hour my bright prospects came to call.
A mockery of silver-plate prosperity
My wedding date, penny-pinched day
Of small battles and economies
That only a sudden sun
Piercing dank December
Could make a summer marriage from,
Life's skimpy ceremonies.

"Envy!" her eyes crinkle in false despair.
"No one has more than me." She dreams
Of mansions and fortunes forever not hers.
It's not a matter of Katmandu or Marrakech
Or seeing homely America by Greyhound bus,
Or even real estate: jewels, never!

Rather, she has never known this world,
Never traded in the marketplace she loves.
And today, now that her name is old at last,
My love of her becomes lessened hate.
We are together in this fleshly fate.

¶

Miracle Man

R eb, your old stereotype mother,
  Unbelievable bubbe bathed you
Once too often in ego ungent,
Praising "my son" so loud
That heaven stopped to listen
With beeswax ears.
On this day of holiness, your yarmulke
Slips like Huck's cap over
Slit thirty-year old eyes.
The tassels of your tallis
Braid themselves to the twist
Of your serpentine sermon.
You shake those private parts
Hidden under white garments of your calling.
Your yontif wife crawls reluctantly
To the prescribed copulating bed.
Your male child already sprouts
Smooth satanic wings.
Deaf to this packed house of
Bad-breathed congregants, you threaten
Their muddled mitzvah plans by
Flying off to winter-locked Leningrad,
Where Russia's only Torah was burned.
So go. Give God and logic the slip—
Meshuggeners deserve each other.

¶

Birthday Letter
"Il faut d'abord durer."

Descendant of November's moody line,
My Wednesday child full of woe,
Who delivered up on a day of
Mizzling rain, mean unopened skies.
The night before I found the secret place
Where neonates slept in sodden sleep,
And carried you, my over-ripe fruit,
Into the laborious drama of your day.
You leapt, a mewing thing, under hot lights,
Flesh and scalded dream in subsided scream.

This year with its freight of sorrow,
We see flesh fold back to earth.
Your old dog sighs in her limited dream
Of dung and bones; the postman brings
Messages from strangers,
The household current complain.
Suburban lights burn lower
And we survive in separate gardens
Of inner space, the private realm
At peace with few invasions.

Now, upon the tightrope of your years
You can acrobat it a bit,
Pull from tension wires
Some somersault of wit:
For what is said is true,
No one can quite get out of it.

❡

At A Neighbor's Funeral

When we met, young mothers of bright babes,
    mortgaged to cracker houses,
  saddled by Spartan ways,
  my bones predicted this day.
Your years played Helen in some Hollywood Troy,
    vain as the peahen preening dull plumage
    into golden-green empurpled female.
That first summer you went berserk
    when Santa Ana winds stunned the land,
    filled contented oases with the fury
    of mind-breaking furnace blast.
Your head came off in the hospital
    of white gown drivel and voltage shock,
    drowned in harmless slipper patter.
Your return to the malice of the street
    heralded the loud ado of "artiste"—
    those daubed works of haunted still lives,
    your shrill ego shrieked against the world's will,
    your prayer wheels spun songs of success.
Yet here in the cradle of your open casket,
    I take the arrow of your being to my breast.
Too tender the spirit, too heavy the burden
    intones the hired religious who can't fool
    us griefless ladies in the winter light.

No one can pronounce your choice of suicide
    though we know the tongue of abomination.
Now, no longer the simple singing grass,
    the single eye of scrutinizing sky.
Now, remain forever in your heavy bronze bed,
    carmined into a suburban Cleopatra
    to sleep long in the anonymous dusk.

¶

Apollo

We caught the last flight out
  Behind the riding wing;
Some passengers flexed with fear,
Others lax with boredom
Carefully embalmed in the take-off gloom;
Well rehearsed we screamed toward the moon,
Full-cheeked in her blinding phase.

We possess it now, that hermaphroditic
Creature, time's curiosity:
The music of the spheres though less ethereal
Proves Newton right, his calculations real.

In white lunar jackets they floated down,
Released madmen from an institution
Or slow-motion skydivers on a mission.
They scouted and routed, conquering there
Among dumb mountains, mute mares.

Through burning equations, beyond evasion,
Our small self seed blooms in this bright sphere.
The dark earth quickens, a new ear listens
To ignorant old gods stumbling in fear.

¶

At The Exhibit

H ere both love gaping and agape agree
   That nothing finally is quite free:
The oiled street, the almost fleshly face
Cost Vincent his ear—it was his ace.
Brothers and sisters in perspiring chance
Edge at vision's elbow, for each a glance
To pass the jostling summer noon
With corny feet and fatigue's swoon.
In the smell of body's press, the black guard
Look past Cezanne's Blue Night, Rousseau's pard.
These borrowed goods from Leningrad
Say "How long is art, life how sad."

¶

Into Morning

T he plumbing's song rings out a five:
"I never think about life,
I think about everything else."
Clever he to wed with words
Before they bed in odorous play,
Sinewy satyr grappling his
Gone-to-flesh sylph in parody
Off some urn from Mycenae.
Still, behind the dawn-blind shades
The flute-miming bird pipes
and mocks them into day.

¶

Horses Of The Night

O lente, lente currite noctis equi."
Far from your drear dreaming island place
You cried to flashing seas, new burning sky,
Metamorphosed as man of this new race.
Childishly we played with time, with hours,
While others gambling for swift happiness
Won quick rewards from simple powers.
But we upright, eschewing easy bliss
Made metaphysical finds on far-flung seas.
Our souls, poor ships, sought ports of agape
Foundered in heavy storms, caught on far reefs.
We outran the wind, the night into this day.
It is late—time's running horses yet fly
Bearing the dark gods' car 'gainst the dark sky.

¶

A Question

What was the greeting faithless Helen found
Returning from her trial at Ilium,
Did old Menelaus accept her calmly back,
And were their unslept sheets newly warmed
By declining tired fevers of primal act?
Did she, of part-goddess, know a woman's fear,
Thinking on her lover gone, her life's huge lack,
That all her stubborn passion was in vain,
Solved nothing, proved neither love nor lover
Could more than tremble the world, cause pain
From willful lust and wild possession
Would come to a winter's dreaming ache
Or some schoolboy's dull copybook lesson?

¶

Gettysburg

Worn by the Union's needs
   he rode rails past summered lands,
  hills sterile after battle stain
  and thought out loud on foolscap sheet:
  apocryphal that those commissioned
  words were set down half by chance?
Almost winter there on the plain
  where the previous orator took the long wind
  and within tradition declaimed
  how sweetly becoming death is:
But he must dictate an older truth,
  of dust and dawn for folk who wait,
  increase, know earth, wake with stars,
  devote each day to common dedications.
He had come to explain the cause of battle won
  to those who would forever know its loss.
The tired cramped voice rose to a snow-flagged sky—
  November on the orchards, long-sloped land
  as his words fell inaudibly among
  the thousands who scarcely listened,
  who found the rhetoric poor, it is said,
  and scarcely knew his speech was through
  before its inviolate cadences had begun.

¶

Die Zeitung

I know, I know the news burns low
 To tell us what we already know:
The battered babe, the jailed addict,
Fires rage in false-toothed attic.
Taxes unzipper every pocket
Undertakers make their deathly profit,
Politicians plant a poison ivy,
Confuse the two-eyed citizenry.
Greasy tills pilfered by greasy hands,
Wars flame up in atlas lands.
Lies pour down like leaves of autumn,
All is Denmark, all is rotten.
I know, I know the news burns low.

❧

Off The Miramar

Death by drowning? Sealore and stuff of tempest,
  My heart thrives in the long-limbed sea,
Rapt eye of tumbling sky and
Murderous water in moment met.
I choose some clever sharp adieu,
Exit easy to the nodding gods:
Not the convalescent shrunken self,
Drugged, duped in hopeless bout
Of skeletaled self and calcified soul,
Monkeyed by tubes and drains,
While vision concentrates on
Triumphant flesh and mind on-off flickers
In patient, viewless stare.
Keep me from the embalmer's art,
Form falsified with sweet flowers,
Music empty, inorganic, the kiss
Some final fragrant breath brought to
Chilly last things badly uttered.
I choose the leap of cannon's boom,
Of hissing, lashing undertow, 'till baptized
With gritty waters that shrive and wash
And forever thrive, I am loosed, fretted no more,
Swimming lost miles past the gulled shore.

¶

January First

Returning to the blank-eyed year
From black lava vacation isles
That grow from pacific blue blindness,
I stood frozen in the snow-slapped airdrome,
Aloha bag and fresh pineapple
Dying in my northern hands.
At home, surly crows bark, black my eyes
Through cycle of mop, broom, sink.
I set teeth on edge in prayer for change:
Deities, powers of heaven and hell
Bring a new circlet of fortune,
Unstick the gears of rusted decades,
Make free the engines of desire,
Explode in unrehearsed surprise.
But I was caught, supernumerary
In the only rehearsed part I knew,
Awoke from my private nutshell of grief
To wish the stars ecliptically back again,
To new moon to return to my days, simple and plain.

¶

Self Portrait
The basement ladies room,
Royce Hall, UCLA

Mirror, mirror in unsilvered glass,
Who was fairest three decades past?
Here is my altered self, spent roses
Lily turning dark, back to earth.

Friends and foes, smart carping crows,
startled I hold title in Academe,
low rung of the fugitive word,
cast me in the verb's past perfect,
leather notebook of lizard skin.

In gray classes scheduled with athletes,
brutish to schoolmarm perfume,
the young sleep under digression's clouds,
their futures push on past Pluto.

Once, I ruled this Roman fortress,
queen of language's royal survey,
decked in cashmere, cultured pearls,
beset by Sophocles, ah, luminous Keats.

Now, the tired gold of my wedding ring
thins to the noon song of carillons;
my hands spotted like a toad,
my head of glory going thin.

And I repeat "old" and "olden"
    in praise of backseat love, simple sin.
    In passions ambered under stars,
    I follow footnotes' traces,
    embrace thin truths and newer fiction.

¶

Three Farewells

Dunkel ist das Leben, ist der Tod.

—The Song of the Earth

I

This side of the dark running river
    I called last to you who floundered,
Cradled the talk in selfish silence
And broke the lifeline, that tenuous knot.
We women talked, made kit kit
Of blood and generation.
July blazed forth in hot Americana,
The tri-colored belief you both saluted until
Your flag flapped windless in empty sky.

On your afternoon of highest meridian,
Somewhere in the wrought Spanish manor,
Your grandson tucked into his nap,
Your children busy with wrapt waking sleep,
The verities of food and music and gold.
All out, turned away.
All out, without knowing or seeing
Without fault.
Until wild rescuers with riotous screams
Violated your drift of pure flotation.
You swam uprooted, faces of dead water lilies,
Drifted in emerald-blue waters.
The curtain will not come down, nor silence descend
Until the mind's home movies unroll,
And obituary language fails.

He: MIT graduate, holder of honors, patents,
       married in funny swashbuckler uniform with
       Depression gin in Grandma's bathtub; proud Puck of a man, given
       through his years to useful
       gimmicks, peculiar adorations.

She: We were married forty years almost to this day.
       I do not swim, but have rented a cabana on
       the lake; gentle, crippled by hopes, far from
       schoolgirl prizes, her diamond rings played
       glissandos on the bought-on-time piano:
       she shall have music wherever she goes.
We pass through ordinary defiles,
The miles of many Mondays.
Here at this pacific resort   —
You would "adore" the camel palms,
Giraffe eucalyptus trees,
The lisp of the punctual sea.
Still honor burns to punctuate your tale,
To round off life's endless sentence.
I see you preserved in the waxworks
Of innocence, of unfocused loves
Too simply defined.

At home with the world's sweet beliefs,
You dwell now in the unheroic pantheon of us all.

II

You took the fastback road out,
Driving past crumbling adobe towns,
Stirring up the Mexican dust; the hour
Turned finicky purple, preying twilight.
Accidentally you lost the track,
Bruised into an over-ripe cantaloupe,
Pobrecita, jolted at your last moment
Into some spasm of holy light.

Now you lie, young and fair among flowers:
Your daughter, blessed womb fruit
As pale an Ophelia who ever slept
Sleeps now coffin-to-coffin,
"Mother" spelled in mortuary splendor.
Your tinted hair and rosy lips perfected
For this grand occasion, your one-night show
Opening and closing on star-stilled eyes.

Looking down on twin embalmed bodies,
I do not wince or turn aside.
I notice we are all working to this place.
The just-shaven priest counts the decades
The Marys hail senseless as snowflakes
Falling upon the statued mourners
Kneeling in stony honor.
He stutters outside tradition, mute
Before what remains most common, most strange,
Seeking a saving poem for your alterered forms,
Saying in his insufficient prayer
Life must be sufficient to life.

III

Uncle Iz sold shoes numberlessly paired
In the family store set among tame plains
In a prison town slightly south of Chicago.
He sang English music hall songs for occasions
Like bar mitzvahs, great family gatherings.
His own fiftieth wedding anniversary,
Goldenly re-enacted was a faithful mock marriage
With new vows and toasts, some dancing.
His wife's urine would etch glass,
One nephew alleged, sipping champagne.

That day his daughter sobbed with great heart
On the hot cemetery slope.
His son, the doctor, stood strictly stoic,
Some mellow-fruit voice rabbi spoke about
Israeli bonds and community service.
It made no sense to lay kind simple Iz
Into that thousand-dollar box, bronzed against
Moisture, dissolution, all change.

ﭏ

Possessor Of The House

Neither buyer nor seller owns this property;
Today unruly April reigns in pettish signs,
    windy cries
To test the realm of vision realized
But you, master builder, lying among rank weeds,
Deserting your schedule of payments and fees.
You own the smallest lot in long-grassed
Singing silence while your finished craft
Commands its hill, wide eyed to complex skies.
The grieving, widowed land homages your skill
Of wood and brick, auger and drill
And glass that holds the seasons, the sun.
We then hold a long promissory note
To hunt the blueprint of your vision,
Possessor of the house.

ſ

Memoriam

May, 1975

I n your portrayal of us all,
Frail, foolish but human still
In those purring cats and raucous birds,
Your stumbling myopic bumbler
Lent us license to endure, to shout
Like cavemen crushing rock, "Watch out!"

Abe, you practiced the truth that
One picture's worth a thousand words,
And with your art in grace and glee
You served the gods of laughter, absurd
Presences that make us free.

❡

Odd Tributaries

More than twenty years have passed since writing the first poems in this booklet and submitting them to an obscure contest.

"Gettysburg" took second place in an Arizona State poetry society competition. It illustrates the strange way the creative process works. One August day, I sat down before my ancient Remington to write a series of haiku. The phone interrupted my thinking. A friend desperately needed transportation to pick up some relative at the Burbank Airport.

Sadly, I obliged, returning close to sundown—and dinner time—and the unfinished Japanese-style poems. Suddenly, it was all before me, half fact, half historical fantasy: President Lincoln's need to write a speech to honor those who had died at the brief, bloody Battle of Gettysburg.

I remembered that Lincoln was supposed to have actually composed the speech on a scrap of paper, or even the back of an envelope, on the train down from Washington. But a new scholarly book contradicts this.

I remembered how his "opponent" the renowned scholar and orator, Edward Everett, had talked himself dry in the preceding two hours and how the people must have felt listening to those strings of platitudes and clichés.

Enough said, I wrote my poem in about a quarter of an hour. Perhaps the rime scheme could be more accurate, but let that pass.

The final version suggests the strength of language and how in a bit over 200 words, Lincoln wrote memorable verse that millions have read and memorized.

The following verse reflects my present concern with lung cancer which was diagnosed about three years ago. I've had a very long reprieve for this kind of disease and have tried to reflect on this late-life gift and pass these thoughts on in my verse.

The Turtle Song

Mourning doves thatched their nest
of twigs and twine, the stuff
that frugal birds must use
to make their nid in shades of dun and gray,
woven without success
into the green singing tree,
their only egg sucked dry
by infertility.

Seeing only one of the monogamous two,
    I thought the other had died
    or even deserted in secret solitude.
No so. Since late this spring
    there they were, the elderly pair, picking crumbs
    left by brighter birds:
    the ebony crow, the blue flick of jay.

Isn't it enough to know that singular love
    endures to stay another day?

❡

Mother's Credo

Mother knew the world better than scholars,
doctors, saints.
She went through her days hefting a big bag
   of complaints.
Her bladder filled with gall and foul odor.
"Let them keep their scalpels." No, no never overpower
me, poor old bag lady with old world truths.

Mother was afraid. Knowledge was never power.
She could prove it by her turtle lamp.
Shaped like half a globe,
It threw faint light by which she read
the book of life, as Tolstoy said.
The turtle with its impenetrable armor,
moved never an inch in Mother's 91 years.
Though her world was square she never fell off,
But lived for the last laugh, the final scoff.

¶

The Gift

S kip one generation to discover
You, my younger tender flesh
Costumed in plastic blue and gold
Disney child in let's pretend regale.

The world of tender love, later romance
Will come like the bold prince
You view electronically, but he will come
Boldly outrageous to your white bed
To teach you truths about which
You've only read.

Sweet morsel, a most modern child,
Charged by Wal-Mart's bulging aisles,
Waving your new battery-powered wand,
You step from Cleo's empurpled barge
Mistress of all in your imagined land.

¶

I Lost It At The Movies

Coleridge suspended disbelief,
to find vision in rhythm and rime.
Another "lost it"—her innocence?
    watching midnight "flicks" at a later time.

Shadows of slim girls, hoods and finks,
    cops and robbers escape in the Brinks,
    their dated truck loaded with loot.
"We're in the money, we're in the money, honey."

It doesn't matter—either black or white,
    take me on wings of suspended delight.
I need no color to ease disbelief,
The rich and the poor. The Indian chief.
They laugh, they snicker.
It makes no matter,
They are my flicks of midnight relief.

❡

Let The Night Creep In

"Hush, she has that dread disease
that attacks and takes its due."

I hold no secret; people know all,
I'm going where all must go,
But not this hour or even this day.
Though gossips know my destiny
better than I.

But do they know the real price
Of dying day by day,
Of guessing this may be the final time
To straighten drawers, settle accounts,
Make the last phone calls, pay the bills that mount?

That great thing creeps up on silent feet.
It plays a parlor game: win some, lose some.

No one can cheat it, no one defeat it.
Yes, the world is both square and fair
As it comes to me, to you, to all—everywhere.

❧

A Just Reward

I hate the word "spinster" and even more "old maid."
I hate to know how many
 ambiguous men or doubtful women
 never wed, but somehow pay
 to satisfy their flesh.

Still, it hurts to know no one
 has taken his pleasure from her thickening body
 like the handsome man I once eyed
 in the jewelry store.

He bought a heavy rope of pearls,
 freshwater, glowing in memory
 Of some woman's—possibly his wife's—
 pleasuring him out of everyday senses
 in that anesthesia of delight.

¶

After Her Funeral

I like to think of our last time together
at the alfresco luncheon party,
when the southern skies burned
our fair wrinkled fairness
and turned us tan.

Then you turned on me and to my
polite inquiry about your health,
you almost spat out, "I don't want
to talk to you."

Just anger at our mutual sickness?
or that unknown place where you were going,
your brain ravaged by black tumors and gray fluids.

It was the final thing between us.
I, who might cling to consciousness
a month or part of another year,
I took no umbrage. I understood.

Some called you unreliable, another even thief.
Strong words for a mid-life lady, whose body
had gotten away from imagined perfection,
after husbanding two men and bearing children;
then was required to cash it all in.
Others at yesterday's service were far kinder,
likening you to one who makes mischief and fun
from a generous, overflowing heart.

While I saw you as an unloved child thirsting for care.
A stray puppy with no pedigree, who'd lost its way.

It makes no matter now that you are dust.

¶